129 Greatest Basketball Quotes from the Game's Most Famous People

Adam E. Murray
Copyright 2012

Preface

Nine is considered a good number in Chinese culture because it sounds the same as the word "long-lasting." Nine is strongly associated with the Chinese dragon, a symbol of magic and power.

9 Publishing Company
P.O. Box 14808
Portland, Oregon 97293
9publishingco@gmail.com
www.9publishingco.com

Also by Adam E. Murray:

<u>Football Quotes: 129 Quotes and Sayings from Famous People</u>

<u>Golf Humor: 129 Greatest Golf Quotes from the World's Most Famous People</u>

Table of Contents

Introduction											6

Chapter 1 – Pro Basketball Players						8

Chapter 2 – Basketball Coaches						20

Chapter 3 – Celebrities and Basketball					29

Chapter 4 – Unknown Authors & Basketball			33

Conclusion										35

Introduction

When James Naismith invented the game of basketball in 1891, he couldn't have imagined the soaring popularity and how inventive the game continues to be.

Played on all continents and just about every country on earth, "hoops" provides a ton of athleticism and excitement to players, coaches and fans alike.

With this third book from best-selling author Adam E. Murray, you will find some of the most memorable words ever spoken about the game.

In "129 Greatest Basketball Quotes from the Game's Most Famous People," you will some pure gems you are not soon to forget. From world class athletes like Lebron James and Michael Jordan to coaches like Phil Jackson and John Wooden to celebrities like Zac Effron and Ashley Judd, to writers such as Jim Murray and Dave Barry, you will be taking a deep dive into a vast pool of basketball's greatest messages from this hand-picked collection.

So take a deep breath and relax. You've got 129 gems of basketball that will keep you entertained time and again as you read, chuckle and marvel at "129 Greatest Basketball Quotes from the Game's Most Famous People."

Chapter 1 – What Pro Basketball Players Say About the Game

"I can accept failure, everyone fails at something. But I can't accept not trying."

- *Michael Jordan (1963 -) Pro basketball player*

"One man can be a crucial ingredient on a team, but one man cannot make a team."

- *Kareem Abdul-Jabbar (1947 -) Pro basketball player*

"When I was young, I never wanted to leave the court until I got things exactly correct. My dream was to become a pro."

- *Larry Bird (1956 -) Pro basketball player*

"Good, better, best. Never let it rest. Until your good is better and your better is best."

- *Tim Duncan (1976 -) Pro basketball player*

"I never thought I'd lead the NBA in rebounding, but I got a lot of help from my team-mates – they did a lot of missing."

- *Moses Malone (1955 -) Pro basketball player*

"Me shooting 40% at the foul line is just God's way to say nobody's perfect."

- *Shaquille O'Neal (1972 -) Pro basketball player*

"If you get depressed about being the second-best team in the world, then you've got a problem."

- *Julius Erving (1950 -) Pro basketball player*

"I've learned what it feels like to lose, believe me. But I think, in the end, that is just going to make winning that much better."

- *Kevin Durant (1988 -) Pro basketball player*

"You just bounce back. I promise you if you let this game get to you too much, you won't be able to perform in the next game. ... You just take that game as it is and get ready for the next one. Shoot the same shots. Hopefully, they'll go in."

- Chris Paul (1985 -) Pro basketball player

"We got to win. Win no matter what. Trip, kick somebody, fight, bite. Whatever. Win."

- Derrick Rose (1988 -) Pro basketball player

"Everything negative - pressure, challenges - is all an opportunity for me to rise."

- Kobe Bryant (1978 -) Pro basketball player

"If somebody says no to you, or if you get cut, Michael Jordan was cut his first year, but he came back and he was the best ever. That is what you have to have. The attitude that I'm going to show everybody, I'm going to work hard to get better and better."

- Magic Johnson (1959 -) Pro basketball player

"My heroes are and were my parents. I can't see having anyone else as my heroes."

- Michael Jordan (1963 -) Pro basketball player

"People ask me if I could fly, I said, 'yeah.... for a little while.'"

- Michael Jordan (1963 -) Pro basketball player

"I can do something else besides stuff a ball through a hoop. My biggest resource is my mind."

- Kareem Abdul-Jabbar (1947 -) Pro basketball player

"Durability is part of what makes a great athlete."

- Bill Russell (1934 -) Pro basketball player

"I just think we want to stay healthy, and I don't think we think about a sense of urgency. We realize how old we are, we realize we've been playing this game for a long time, but you know what? We're not done yet."

- Karl Malone (1963 -) Pro basketball player

"Right up until the time I retired at age 37, I felt like there were still things that I could do better."

- Julius Erving (1950 -) Pro basketball player

"I believe that good things come to those who work."

- Wilt Chamberlain (1936 - 1999) Pro basketball player

"The time when there is no one there to feel sorry for you or to cheer for you is when a player is made."

- Tim Duncan (1976 -) Pro basketball player

"A winner is someone who recognizes his God-given talents, works his tail off to develop them into skills, and uses these skills to accomplish his goals."

- Larry Bird (1956 -) Pro basketball player

"Ask me to play. I'll play. Ask me to shoot. I'll shoot. Ask me to pass. I'll pass. Ask me to steal, block out, sacrifice, lead, dominate. ANYTHING. But it's not what you ask of me. It's what I ask of myself."

- Lebron James (1984 -) Pro basketball player

"A lot of late nights in the gym, a lot of early mornings, especially when your friends are going out, you're going to the gym, those are the sacrifices that you have to make if you want to be an NBA basketball player."

- Jason Kidd (1973 -) Pro basketball player

"But the point of using the number was to show that sex was a great part of my life as basketball was a great part of my life. That's the reason why I was single."

- Wilt Chamberlain (1936 - 1999) Pro basketball player

"I started out as a football player. I liked to inflict pain. In basketball, it was the same thing."

- Shaquille O'Neal (1972 -) Pro basketball player

"I think I started learning lessons about being a good person long before I ever knew what basketball was. And that starts in the home, it starts with the parental influence."

- Julius Erving (1950 -) Pro basketball player

"I think that basketball players should get the job done no matter how it looks on the screen."

- Oscar Robertson (1938 -) Pro basketball player

"I'm not a role model... Just because I dunk a basketball doesn't mean I should raise your kids."

- Charles Barkley (1963 -) Pro basketball player

"I'm the basketball version of a gravedigger."

- Dennis Rodman (1961 -) Pro basketball player

"If all I'm remembered for is being a good basketball player, then I've done a bad job with the rest of my life."

> *- Isaiah Thomas (1961 -) Pro basketball player*

"If I weren't earning $3 million a year to dunk a basketball, most people on the street would run in the other direction if they saw me coming."

> *- Charles Barkley (1963 -) Pro basketball player*

"Once I grew from 6'1" to about 6'6", by that time I was going into 12th grade, and that's when I started wanting to play basketball, because, pretty much basketball players always got the girl.

> *- Eric Williams (1972 -) Pro basketball player*

"When I dunk, I put something on it. I want the ball to hit the floor before I do."

> *- Darryl Dawkins (1957 -) Pro basketball player*

"Talent wins games, but team work and intelligence wins championships."

> *- Michael Jordan (1963 -) Pro basketball player*

"The best teams have chemistry. They communicate with each other and they sacrifice personal glory for the common goal."

- Dave DeBusschere (1940 - 2003) Pro basketball player

"I tell kids to pursue their basketball dreams, but I tell them to not let that be their only dream."

- Kareem Abdul-Jabbar (1947 -) Pro basketball player

"As far as carrying the torch for the years to come, I don't know. I just want to be the best basketball player I can be."

- Kobe Bryant (1978 -) Pro basketball player

"The idea is not to block every shot. The idea is to make your opponent believe that you might block every shot."

- Bill Russell (1934 -) Pro basketball player

"The only difference between a good shot and a bad shot is if it goes in or not."

- Charles Barkley (1963 -) Pro basketball player

"Don't let what other people think decide who you are."

- Dennis Rodman (1961 -)

"I have missed more than 9000 shots in my career. I have lost almost 300 games. On 26 occasions I have been entrusted to take the game winning shot...and missed. And I have failed over and over and over again in my life. And that is why... I succeed."

- Michael Jordan (1963 -) Pro basketball player

"The rule was "No autopsy, no foul."

- Stewart Granger (1961 -) Pro basketball player

"I would tell players to relax and never think about what's at stake. Just think about the basketball game. If you start to think about who is going to win the championship, you've lost your focus."

- Michael Jordan (1963 -) Pro basketball player

"They say that nobody is perfect. Then they tell you practice makes perfect. I wish they'd make up their minds."

- Wilt Chamberlain (1936 - 1999) Pro basketball player

"Kids are great. That's one of the best things about our business, all the kids you get to meet. It's a shame they have to grow up to be regular people and come to the games and call you names."

- Charles Barkley (1963 -) Pro basketball player

"Everybody pulls for David, nobody roots for Goliath."

- Wilt Chamberlain (1936 - 1999) American basketball player

"Love never fails; Character never quits; and with patience and persistence; Dreams do come true."

- Pete Maravich (1947 - 1988) Pro basketball player

"Everybody on a championship team doesn't get publicity, but everyone can say he's a champion."

- Magic Johnson (1959 -) Pro basketball player

"Obstacles don't have to stop you. If you run into a wall, don't turn around and give up. Figure out how to climb it, go through it, or work around it."

- Michael Jordan (1963 -) Pro basketball player

"Push yourself again and again. Don't give an inch until the final buzzer sounds."

    - Larry Bird (1956 -) Pro basketball player

"You can't get much done in life if you only work on the days when you feel good."

    - Jerry West (1938 -) Pro basketball player

"Some people want it to happen, some wish it would happen, others make it happen."

    - Michael Jordan (1963 -) Pro basketball player

"Do your best when no one is looking. If you do that, then you can be successful in anything that you put your mind to."

    - Bob Cousy (1928 -) Pro basketball player

"We win because we play together as a team."

    - John Havlicek (1940 -) Pro basketball player

"I'm like Rudolph the Red-Nosed Reindeer. If I'm not ready, the sled isn't going to go."

- Kevin Garnett (1976 -) Pro basketball player

Chapter 2 – What Basketball Coaches Say About the Game

"For an athlete to function properly, he must be intent. There has to be a definite purpose and goal if you are to progress. If you are not intent about what you are doing, you aren't able to resist the temptation to do something else that might be more fun at the moment."

- John Wooden (1910 - 2010) College basketball coach

"In basketball – as in life – true joy comes from being fully present in each and every moment, not just when things are going your way. Of course, it's no accident that things are more likely to go your way when you stop worrying about whether you're going to win or lose and focus your full attention on what's happening right this moment."

- Phil Jackson (1945 -) Pro basketball coach

"A basketball team is like the five fingers on your hand. If you can get them all together, you have a fist. That's how I want you to play."

- Mike Krzyzewski (1947 -) College basketball coach

"Basketball is a team game. But that doesn't mean all five players should have the same amount of shots."

   - *Dean Smith (1931 -) College basketball coach*

"Basketball is like war in that offensive weapons are developed first, and it always takes a while for the defense to catch up."

   - *Red Auerbach (1917 - 2006) Pro basketball coach*

"I've tried to handle winning well, so that maybe we'll win again, but I've also tried to handle failure well. If those serve as good examples for teachers and kids, then I hope that would be a contribution I have made to sport. Not just basketball, but to sport."

   - *Mike Krzyzewski (1947 -) College basketball coach*

"You don't play against opponents, you play against the game of basketball."

   - *Bobby Knight (1940 -) College basketball coach*

"A basketball team is like the five fingers on your hand. If you can get them all together, you have a fist. That's how I want you to play."

- Mike Krzyzewski (1947 -) College basketball coach

"Winning is like deodorant - it comes up and a lot of things don't stink."

- Doc Rivers (1961 -) Pro basketball coach

"Fans never fall asleep at our games, because they're afraid they might get hit by a pass."

- George Raveling (1937 -) College basketball coach

"We're shooting 100 percent - 60 percent from the field and 40 percent from the free-throw line."

- Norm Stewart (1935 -) College basketball coach

"We have a great bunch of outside shooters. Unfortunately, all our games are played indoors."

- Weldon Drew (???) College basketball coach

"Talent is God given. Be humble. Fame is man-given. Be grateful. Conceit is self-given. Be careful."

- John Wooden (1910 - 2010) College basketball coach

"Be a dreamer. If you don't know how to dream, you're dead."

    - Jim Valvano (1946 - 1993) College basketball coach

"Never give up! Failure and rejection are only the first step to succeeding."

    - Jim Valvano (1946 - 1993) College basketball coach

"Prepare for every game like you just lost your last game."

    - Lon Kruger (1952 -) College basketball coach

"There's no such thing as coulda, shoulda, or woulda. If you shoulda and coulda, you woulda done it."

    - Pat Riley (1945 -) Pro basketball coach

"I asked a ref if he could give me a technical foul for thinking bad things about him. He said, of course not. I said, well, I think you stink. And he gave me a technical. You can't trust em."

    - Jim Valvano (1946 - 1993) College basketball coach

"You have no choices about how you lose, but you do have a choice about how you come back and prepare to win again."

- Pat Riley (1945 -) Pro basketball coach

"Don't let what you cannot do interfere with what you can do."

- John Wooden (1910 - 2010) College basketball coach

"Good teams become great ones when the members trust each other enough to surrender the Me for the We."

- Phil Jackson (1945 -) Pro basketball coach

"I always tried to make clear that basketball is not the ultimate. It is of small importance in comparison to the total life we live. There is only one kind of life that truly wins, and that is the one that places faith in the hands of the Savior. Until that is done, we are on an aimless course that runs in circles and goes nowhere."

- John Wooden (1910 - 2010) College basketball coach

"Basketball is a game that gives you every chance to be great, and puts every pressure on you to prove that you haven't got what it takes. It never takes away the chance, and it never eases up on the pressure."

   - *Bob Sundvold (1955 -) College basketball coach*

"The most important key to achieving great success is to decide upon your goal and launch, get started, take action, move."

   - *John Wooden (1910 - 2010) College basketball coach*

"Basketball is like war in that offensive weapons are developed first, and it always takes a while for the defense to catch up."

   - *Red Auerbach (1917 - 2006) Pro basketball coach*

"It is most difficult, in my mind, to separate any success, whether it be in your profession, your family, or as in my case, in basketball, from religion."

   - *John Wooden (1910 - 2010) College basketball coach*

"If you meet the Buddha in the lane, feed him the ball."

   - *Phil Jackson (1945 -) Pro basketball coach*

"There are times **I get mad** and want to strangle somebody, and then I go to Mass and say, Stop me from having this feeling that I want to absolutely punch this guy in the face. I'm from Pittsburgh. You come at me? I come at you twice. You hurt one of mine? I'm burning your village."

- John Calipari (1959 -) College basketball coach

"When I went to Catholic high school in Philadelphia, we just had one coach for football and basketball. He took all of us who turned out and had us run through a forest. The ones who ran into the trees were on the football team."

- George Raveling (1937 -) College basketball coach

"The secret is to have eight great players and four others who will cheer like crazy."

-Jerry Tarkanian (1930 -) College basketball coach

"What you are as a person is far more important that what you are as a basketball player."

- John Wooden (1910 - 2010) College basketball coach

"You can run a lot of plays when your X is twice as big as the other guys' O. It makes your X's and O's pretty good."

- Paul Westphal (1950 -) Pro basketball coach

"There are really only two plays: Romeo and Juliet, and put the darn ball in the basket."

- Abe Lemons (1922 - 2002) College basketball coach

"If you make every game a life and death proposition, you're going to have problems. For one thing, you'll be dead a lot."

- Dean Smith (1931 -) College basketball coach

"Failure is good. It's fertilizer. Everything I've learned about coaching I've learned from making mistakes."

- Rick Pitino (1952 -) College basketball coach

"It's what you get from games you lose that is extremely important."

- Pat Riley (1945 -) Pro basketball coach

"Coaching is easy. Winning is the hard part."

- Elgin Baylor (1934 -) Pro basketball player & NBA executive

"He who controlleth the backboard, controlleth the game."

   - Adolph Rupp (1901 - 1977) College basketball coach

"Winning is overrated. The only time it is really important is in surgery and war."

   - Al McGuire (1928 - 2001) College basketball coach

"We try to stress the little things because little things lead to big things."

   - Steve Alford (1964 -) College basketball coach

"Those who work the hardest are the last to surrender."

   - Rick Pitino (1952 -) College basketball coach

"Don't give up, don't ever give up."

   - Jim Valvano (1946 - 1993) College basketball coach

Chapter 3 – What Celebrities Say About the Game

"Giving "Magic" the basketball is like giving Hitler an army, Jesse James a gang, or Genghis Khan a horse."

- Jim Murray (1919 - 1998) American sportswriter

"Be strong in body, clean in mind, lofty in ideals."

- James Naismith (1861 - 1939) Inventor game of basketball

"And it blew my mind when I started to get wind of the fact that they actually liked me being around. That was humbling, because Kentucky basketball is a big deal, and I am not the biggest fan - I am just the most notorious one."

- Ashley Judd (1968 -) American actress

"And my father didn't have money for me to go to college. And at that particular time they didn't have black quarterbacks, and I don't think I could have made it in basketball, because I was only 5' 11". So I just picked baseball."

- Willie Mays (1931 -) American baseball player

"As all of us with any involvement in sports knows, no two umpires or no two referees have the same strike zone or call the same kind of a basketball game."

- Herb Kohl (1935 -) American owner pro basketball team

"Every little kid that steps on the court or the field has aspirations to go pro. I think being a pro basketball player is the best job. The thing I had to realize was that I can't do every dream that I have."

- Brian McKnight (1969 -) American songwriter

"Hockey is a sport for white men. Basketball is a sport for black men. Golf is a sport for white men dressed like black pimps."

- Tiger Woods (1975 -) Professional golfer

"I always dreamt of being a basketball player. A dream that only I believed in."

- David Duchovny (1960 -) American actor

"I am sure that no man can derive more pleasure from money or power than I do from seeing a pair of basketball goals in some out of the way place."

- James Naismith (1861- 1939) Inventor game of basketball

"I've got a basketball signed by all the greats from Julius Irving to Oscar Robinson. It was at an All Star game I got them all to sign it. So that ain't going nowhere. I'm going to die with that in my casket."

- Ice Cube (1969 -) American musician

"In football, there were drinks available everywhere you looked. On a golf tournament, you could find one free anywhere you wanted it. In tennis and NBA basketball, everybody had a hospitality suite, and so you could go there and load up if you wanted to."

- Pat Summerall (1930 -) American sportscaster

"In sixth grade, my basketball team made it to the league championships. In double overtime, with three seconds left, I rebounded the ball and passed it - to the wrong team! They scored at the buzzer and we lost the game. To this day, I still have nightmares!"

- Zac Efron (1987 -) American actor

"It took me a while to realize that basketball wasn't football."

- Merlin Olsen (1940 - 2010) Professional football player

"Magic Johnson, former basketball player, may run for mayor of LA in the next election. Remember the good 'ol days when only qualified people ran for office like actors and professional wrestlers."

- Jay Leno (1950 -) American TV host

"This is the second most exciting indoor sport, and the other one shouldn't have spectators."

- Dick Vertlieb (1930 - 2008) NBA executive

"I haven't been able to slam-dunk the basketball for the past five years. Or, for the thirty-eight years before that, either."

- Dave Barry (1947 -) Newspaper columnist

"We can't win at home and we can't win on the road. My problem as general manager is I can't think of another place to play."

- Pat Williams (1940 -) NBA executive

Chapter 4 – What Unknown Authors Say About the Game

"Basketball doesn't build character it reveals it."

- Author unknown

"My responsibility is getting all my players playing for the name on the front of the jersey, not the one on the back."

- Author unknown

"Basketball doesn't build character it reveals it."

- Author unknown

"If you think small things don't matter, think of the last game you lost by one point."

- Author unknown

"It is not how big you are, it is how big you play."

- Author unknown

"On any given night, anyone can beat anyone."

- Author unknown

"Losers quit when they're tired. Winners quit when they've won."

- Author unknown

"Teamwork: The fuel that produces uncommon results in common people."

- Author unknown

"Those who have invested the most are the last to surrender."

- Author unknown

Conclusion

Thanks for your purchase of this eBook. My intention with this third sports collection and "129 Greatest Basketball Quotes from the Game's Most Famous People," is to share with you some brilliant, witty and powerful anecdotes you can read by yourself or share with fellow hoops fans.

This collection will continue to grow. Feel free to send favorites of yours to the email address in the front of the book to be added in later editions.

Here's to the great game invented by James Naismith more than a century ago!

Would you do me a favor? Give my book a review by visiting the Amazon page at the link below. It would be greatly appreciated.

<http://www.amazon.com/dp/B007V6INKU>

Thank you,
Adam E. Murray

Made in United States
Orlando, FL
18 December 2023